consumer power

[a digital revolution]

Susan Frederick

First printed in the United States April 2001
Updated version printed November 2014

ISBN 978-0-692-33160-6

Library of Congress Control Number 2001089775

Dedicated to Matt & Jordan—
and to every one in the world who dares
to pursue their highest dream...

From one who is sharing in that journey.

"TICK-TOCK, THE GAME IS LOCKED

AND NOBODY ELSE CAN PLAY!"

When we were growing up, we used that sing-song taunt to keep out any playmates we wanted to exclude. We just "locked the game" so they couldn't play.

In the traditional world of everyday commerce, the consumer has been odd man out. We're the ones creating the profit—ALL of it, as a matter of fact. We're the workers and the buyers. But at the end of the day, somehow all the profit winds up somewhere else. For decades, that's been okay with us. We went home with our purchases and never gave a second thought to how the profits got divvied up among the players.

But as our buddy Bob Dylan sang a generation ago—the times they are a'changing. With an economy in free-fall things begin to look a whole lot different. Some of us woke up to this a long time ago—and some of us are just now waking up. But once it dawns on you that this thing called free enterprise is a VERY big game—one that *we ourselves are financing, yet without being included in the profit loop*—a lot of things crazy things begin to make sense.

For example, it makes sense that when consumers are left out of the profit loop, an economic bump in the road can become a recession, or even a depression. Think about it. If our jobs pay us at below wholesale (which they do) but our cost of living is retail (which it is)—how can that equation possibly work? It doesn't. So it's no surprise that year after year the results we get on a personal level are deficit and debt (credit card balances that grow hair)—and at a city, state, and national level, the same—on steroids.

Why? The game is locked. And the rule of the game is simple:

Everybody gets paid when people buy, except the people who are buying.

But it doesn't have to be that way. There is a way to unlock the game and balance the equation. In fact, it's the only way I see that consumers like you and me can rise up, one by one, join our hands and hearts, and take back our future.

I call it Consumer Power. Want to play?

TABLE OF CONTENTS

PREFACE

This is a true story. Not even the names are changed to protect the innocent. In a way, that makes it personal. But I'm just one of thousands of people who have found our financial options to be radically different from what we had expected them to be. Some of us for better, some for worse.

I'm a single parent, widowed and divorced. Two marriages, two bittersweet attempts at happily ever after. Two wonderful children, Matt and Jordan, one from each marriage, carry on the sweetness of those dreams into the next generation. I am very blessed to know those two; to have the privilege of sharing life with them. And I'm very grateful to have shared even more of that because I haven't had to have a job for many years. That's because I became a part of an entrepreneurial experiment.

I call it an experiment because none of us really knew it would turn out this good.

We thought it was a good idea, like Bill Gates thought Windows was a good idea, and Ray Kroc thought fast food was a good idea, and Sam Walton thought that cutting out the middle man and passing on the savings to consumers was a good idea.

But none of us knew where it could take us. We tried to imagine. And we believed. But there was no way to *know*. No one ever knows. Everything astounding is an act of faith. And we had faith. (Some days more than others.)

Nevertheless, it was a drastic shift of thinking for me in the business realm. As a business broker, I understood business in a traditional way. Manufacturers, jobbers, wholesalers, retailers—I worked with them all. I knew their griefs, their obligations, their frustrations. And I was the one they called when they decided they would like to pass them on to someone else. I helped them find that someone. I helped that someone make a deal and move on into ownership as smoothly and as unobtrusively as possible.

As for consumers—they were just the last link in the food chain. I didn't think of them at all except when I examined profit and loss statements. That's where they showed up for me. Consumers were the clients: The people who came in the door for products or for service and kept the money machine cranking. During the day, they were "the other guys," the ones I *didn't* work with. But when I came home at night (some nights later than others) I was one of them.

We all are. We can't help it. Toothpaste, dog food, shaving crème, shampoo, toilet paper, razor blades, birthday presents, graduation presents, Christmas presents, clothes, appliances—you name it—we buy it. We never think about what happens to our money once we plunk it down over the counter. It's gone. That's all we know. We go home with our stuff and that's the end of it.

Tomorrow we go back to work to make some money to buy more. It's my story. It's your story. But it's not over yet. There's another chapter. And it's a great one. Here's hoping you choose to join us for—the rest of the story.

Introduction

A New Kind of Income:
Passive Consumer Residuals

T ime is money, right? That's what they told me. And for most of my working life, I would have sworn it was true. I mean, wouldn't you? Which one of us hasn't put in our time, slugging away, trying to make ends meet and find a little left over for a few optional things? Sometimes there wasn't quite enough for those optional things. That's why the credit card balance didn't get paid off every month—or any month—for some of us hardworking consumers.

As an employee, if you want more money—it takes more time. And where do you get more of that?

Maybe you can tweak up the pay a little with more education—but then again, you may already be one of the more educated among us. But if you have a car payment, a mortgage payment, and a balance on your credit card (or more than one), you're paddling the time and money canoe alongside all the rest of us, well educated or not.

If you haven't read Robert Kiyosaki's best selling books by now, I highly recommend them. It's no surprise to me that all of them have been on Wall Street Journal's best seller list at the same time. *Rich Dad, Poor Dad* is the story of two ways of thinking. One that leads to riches, the other to the kind of poverty we've come to know as mediocrity. *The Cash Flow Quadrant* is about four kinds of income and the emotional IQ of those who live in each of those four quadrants. *Rich Dad's Guide to Investing* is a mental travelogue of how to make the journey from broke to wealthy in a way that changes more than just your check book balance.

The Cash Flow Quadrant shows you the four kinds of income. The two on the left side (**E** & **S**) require endless amounts of time. If you're Employed or **S**elf-employed, you're familiar with that kind of income. (It was someone in one of those two quadrants who coined the expression "time is money," because in those two quadrants, that's exactly right.)

In the third quadrant (**B**), the cashflow comes from **B**usiness systems that can operate without the owner's presence. Systems like the one Ray Kroc developed which became McDonald's Corporation or Sam Walton's network of discount stores are well known examples of that kind of income. In this case, it's not *time* that creates the money—it's the *System* that produces it.

The last quadrant is the Investor's quadrant (**I**), where money invested in other businesses produces more money. The most successful **I**'s always come from the **B** quadrant, rather than the **E** or **S,** since most E's and S's don't understand the right side of the quadrant or they'd be over there themselves.

So there are four quadrants with three kinds of income: Cashflow that comes from *time.* Cashflow that comes from *systems.* And cashflow that comes from *money.*

But there's a whole new kind of income on the horizon. Like most of life's amazing phenomena, it didn't come galloping over the hill full grown. It has evolved slowly— even painfully—over decades. Call it *passive consumer residual* income. If you reference the Cash Flow Quadrant, you won't see it there. That's because it's a new breed, a different kind of animal. It's a hybrid—a combination of the two right-side quadrants, **B** and **I.** It's an income stream that makes use of a Business System, all right, but the Investment it involves is simply a redirection of money you're already spending as a consumer; things you use every day and will continue to use for the rest of your life. It's a business system that optimizes your consumer power.

Consumer power. We've always had it. We just didn't know we did. And we certainly didn't have a clue how to organize it for profit. But fifty years ago we didn't know how to use personal computers either—or the Internet. Today we do. And the business model that's evolving is a revolutionary idea whose time has finally come.

I was part of the "pilot project," you might say. I was a successful business broker back then—whatever that means. Time starved, hard working, educated—a single parent with two kids, paying the bills and hoping for more—I sat down with a PhD from MIT, a professor of engineering who patiently explained the business model to me. I was graciously skeptical. But I remember wondering, "What if it were possible? What if I could actually create an income by distilling profits from goods and services I'm already paying for? And if it were actually possible, how big could that income stream become? How much consumer power, I wondered, do we really have?"

Today I know the answer.

It's unlimited.

Chapter One

It's *What* That Makes the World Go 'Round?

Love is the quality in life
Money is the process.

One

Whether we like to think so or not, it's not love, but *money* that keeps the world's machinery running. Since it's our medium of exchange for goods and services—when it isn't moving, neither are we. I remember a few years ago when the whole government shut down because Congress couldn't agree on the federal budget. Remember that?

Thousands of people didn't go to work that day. I remember thinking how rapidly serious the economic ripples could get if that stalemate had continued.

So even though we love to sing our songs about love (and it's definitely love that makes us glad we're here)—it's money that keeps things going. And when there isn't enough of it, life can be painful. On the other hand, with a good supply of it, life gets fun. You can be a kid again—with better toys. And what's even more fun—you can make a lot of difference in the lives of other people.

I don't understand the folks who say they don't want more money in their lives, do you? Maybe they mean they don't want a lot more stuff. I can understand that. But money isn't stuff. Sure, it can buy stuff—but it doesn't have to. Money just gives us choices. And it can do a lot of other things besides put more stuff in our lives.

Money extends our personal power. And that can be a good thing. I knew a gentleman once who taught a class I took. He told us he'd found out how to be in more than one place at a time. He said that even though he seemed to be standing in front of us, he was at that very moment turning on the lights in an orphanage in Haiti, and passing out school books to children in private school, and feeding a whole line of homeless people that live downtown. He smiled and asked us if we knew how he could do all that while he was standing there teaching that class. I knew him—so of course I knew the answer. He was using his money to do it. This man with a huge heart had a matching bank account. And together they did marvelous things.

Who wouldn't want more power to make a difference somewhere in the world?

And isn't the best place to start making good things happen right in your own home? Think about it for a second. How long has it been since you spent some major quality time (without the pressure of a deadline) with the special people in your life? Why don't you do it next week? Take the week off. Go somewhere wonderful. Make great things happen. What's stopping you? The boss? The bills? The clients? The bank account?

Isn't your time your own to set your own priorities?

I think it's ironic. They told us time is money—but when you really look at it, *money* is time!

Every one of us has played out our own version of it. When we don't have enough money, we can't do with our time what we'd really like to do with it. But when the money is there, we can hire out what can be done for us so we can do what only *we* can do. No one else can make your spouse—and those kids of yours—feel loved by you. No one but you can do that. It just takes time. The crucial question is—do you have enough of that?

I didn't. Single parents don't have time. They work too much. And not only single parents. So do a lot of other people. Somehow, even though we seem to understand that time is money (on the left side of the quadrant), we don't quite get it that more money would buy back our time. Once I understood that, I knew what had to be done.

But the irony went further. I didn't have time to make more money so I could buy back my time! It was a catch 22—and I was stuck in it, along with millions of others. I prayed for a way out and I kept my antenna up. Surely, there had to be one.

Thank God there was.

Chapter Two

The Excluded Consumer

*An unobserved inequity can
go on for generations. Once
it is observed, however, its
days are numbered.*

Two

So if money makes the world go around, who makes the money go around? *We* do. The Consumers. We create the demand. We buy the stuff. And we foot the bill. When you walk into a grocery store, a drug store, a discount store—who do you think is paying for that light bill? Who's paying those employees? Who's paying all that overhead and that insurance? *We* are!

When you think about it, consumers drive the whole economy. Without us, profit wouldn't exist. There might be manufacturers, middle men, wholesalers and retailers— but without us consumers paying for their salaries and putting profits in the stockholders' pockets, they wouldn't be around too long.

So we're the big cheese, huh? We're the reason it's all happening. But let me ask you this. Of all the people in the profit chain, who's the only one that gets excluded? Manufacturers? Nope, they get their share of the pie. How about the middle men? Are you kidding? They make billions every year. What about the wholesalers and the retailers? They all get their piece of the action. So what about *you*?

"Who me?" Yes *you*.

"I'm just the consumer. I'm the one who buys the stuff and takes it home." And how much profit do you get?

"Profit? I don't get profit." Not any?

"No."

Why not?

"Why should I?"

Because you drive the market. Because without you there *isn't* any market. Because you foot the bill for the whole thing!

"I guess I never thought of that."

Exactly. And *that's* why you're excluded.

It's the oldest story in the human family. If no one notices an inequity, it doesn't change. Well, somebody finally noticed. It wasn't me. Like everybody else, I was totally conditioned. In my world, consumers were the ones who bought things—and everyone got profit from their money except them. That's just how it was. I never questioned it.

I remember when my Great Grandma had her plumbing out behind the house.

She never questioned it. She was conditioned. And when one day she visited my Grandma and saw that she had put the plumbing *in* the house, she wrinkled up her forehead and squinted her blue eyes and shook her head. "I guess you young folks are going to go ahead and do that," she told us. "But it's not for me. I don't think it's natural."

That was the first time I woke up to the power of conditioning.

When I saw the business model for the first time, I felt a lot like my great grandma. I couldn't quite digest that this was happening. I'd never been invited to participate in the profit of any of the products I'd ever bought in my entire life. And over the years—if

I added it up—that represented *lots* of money—everything, in fact, that I had ever made. And suddenly I was viewing a business model that would permanently change that. All I had to lose was my conditioning.

At least I was one up on my great grandma. I was excited.

I knew this was progress. And I *wanted* it to happen. Even if I thought it was too good to actually be true, and I still did—I hoped it was.

Today, quite happily, I'm reconditioned. Now when I remember telling Dr. Hullender it was too good to be true, I smile. Actually, what I had been conditioned to accept was too *bad* to be true—but since nobody knew it back then, I didn't either. One day everyone will know it—just like we all know that putting the plumbing out behind the house is not a good idea. It never was. But we didn't know that till there was a better way.

Including consumers in the profit loop will one day be a standard in the market place. The billions of dollars spent on advertising (much of which is highly suspect anyway) will be gratefully rerouted to consumers who loyally use and promote the products they enjoy. No billboard or TV commercial will ever wield the credibility of a single candid comment from a friend. Word of mouth will always be the best advertising that's available, as well as the most honest. And the only ones who wield that verbal power—are consumers.

So, should we be included in the profit? What do you think?

Chapter Three

The Profitable Community

No man is an island.
But together we can move continents.

Three

So how does it work? Obviously, you can't do it by yourself.

That's right. We're a team. We're organized—at least on paper. Singly, we're not that powerful. But in a group our dollars become hundreds, and the hundreds become thousands. And that's when things begin to happen.

I have a friend who went to the motor bank on her way out of town. It was her vacation and she took her paycheck by to cash it for the trip. She put it in the tube, but when she got the money back, it wasn't the right money. It was someone else's cash and their receipt. So she sent it back. "You must have sent me the wrong money," she told the teller. "This is too much. You need to give me mine."

But the teller wouldn't do it. She'd given my friend's money to another customer and he had driven off, unaware of the mistake. "I can't give you your money until he brings it back," she told my friend.

"Now, wait," my friend objected. "You have my check. It's only right that you give me my money. This is your mistake, not mine."

"Sorry. We'll have to wait," the teller said firmly. "You'll have to come back later."

"You don't understand," my friend persisted. "I'm on my way out of town right now. It's my vacation. And you have my entire paycheck."

Suddenly the fellow in the car next to my friend's car stuck his head out. "What's the problem?" he asked. She told him.

"Okay, let's get organized," he said. So he and my friend explained the situation to the drivers in other lanes. They shut off their engines. "We'll just wait till it gets handled," they told her. "Don't worry."

Within minutes security was on the scene. No cars were moving. The supervisor came out to see what could be done. In a few more minutes my friend had her money. Everyone applauded. Then they started their engines and drove away.

If eight motor bank customers can do that, what can a few hundred consumers do if we all pull together?

Remember, when it comes to profit, we've been left out of the loop—until Now.

But Now is a new day.

Let's assume you take the money you've been spending in the business systems that *exclude you,* and reroute it through a business of your own; one that's connected with other independent business owners in a system that *includes you* as a profit making partner.

How will that benefit you, initially? It depends on how much stuff you buy per month. If you have a big family, you may spend several hundred dollars just on consumables. As you reroute those dollars through your own e-commerce business, you make some profit. For one thing, you get cash back up front. Just a few dollars, but hey, it adds up over time. Last year (2013) all of us consumer power shoppers got back

$2 billion just in cash back. And that doesn't count the back end profit! Remember, you're in business *for* yourself, not *by* yourself. We're creating global teams of independent business owners. Entrepreneurial communities that *connect* their buying power.

Using the connective power of the Internet we build invisible communities—profitable communities not limited by geographical location. We're a community that transcends time and space. Some of us are in Alaska, some in Texas, others in Hawaii, the UK, Canada, Mexico. We connect with people all over the world. We all belong to a community of independent business owners that work together, play together, and make money together. Our motto? *Have fun—Make money—Make a difference!*

Are we an exclusively Internet business? Well, yes we are—and then again, no we're not. We use a lot of different levels of technology to get the job done. Not all of us have a degree in computer literacy. Some of us are still learning how to navigate cyberspace (usually from the kids and grandkids.) We may know how to click and order, but if we run into a problem, we're stuck. So many commercial websites don't even have a number you can call for help (because they don't want you to.) Not so here. If we have a problem or a question there's always someone (yes, indeed, a real live human being) that we can call and talk to. So we're never stuck for long.

So—however techno savvy you are (or are not)—Welcome to our *profitable community*—the Internet revolution that can include us all!

Chapter Four

The Mental Difference

I am my conditioning...
Until I decide I'm not.

Four

Of those who read this book, not everyone will "get it." Some will. Some won't. What separates them? It is a mental difference. Only certain types of thinkers can change their paradigm. Conditioning is a powerful thing—just like it was for my great grandma. Whatever we get used to, even if it's not the best, becomes our comfort zone. And the hardest thing to change is how we think.

Robert Kiyosaki talks a lot about how wealthy people think. They don't think like the rest of us. Bill Gates doesn't think like your friend in the cubicle next door to you at work. There are some differences. And they're important. In fact, they're so important you could say that it's your thinking that creates your life.

All the thoughts you've entertained over the years have brought you to the place you are today—wherever that may be. And it's the thoughts you think from here on out that will take you where you're going, financially and otherwise.

That's a pretty scary thing for most of us. If you're caught in the time trap I was caught in, it's hard to imagine any other way of living. Not that we don't have fantasies of freedom now and then. But fantasies are fantasies. They live in some part of our brain that separates them from reality. They're what we think could not be possible, not really. And so they float around and visit us occasionally, while we continue to create the tangible realities we think we're stuck with.

Years ago, I was a social worker. I worked with parents who'd abused their children. In the process I discovered some things I didn't know before. First of all, I found out people who abuse their kids don't really want to. Most of them aren't mean. They're programmed. They're conditioned. They were abused as kids, themselves. So that's their reference point. It's buried in their brain.

But in my classroom they were open, even eager, to learn new ways to handle their frustrations. They were good students, and we had a lot of fun. I taught them new techniques. Ways to communicate, discipline, and express themselves when they were angry. They came to class for 12 weeks and we all enjoyed it.

Things went fairly well with them, as a rule, the first few weeks after the class was over. But the pattern that eventually emerged was sad. Within a month or two, I'd get a call. It was CPS, Child Protective Services. They wanted me to testify in court. My students, now my friends, had gone back to their old ways. A child was hurt. Parental rights were being terminated. The old conditioning had returned.

That's the devastating power of conditioning. It can take us down. It can rob us of the things we could have had, the happiness we might have found had we been able to get free of it.

And that's true here, as well. What has your financial conditioning been? Is debt a normal thing? Can you imagine realistically a life where you are free to set your own priorities; spend time with the people that you love; and give to the causes that you want to prosper? Or is the future you envision pretty much the same as what you've known so far? It doesn't have to be.

We live in a time of drastic change. Everywhere we look, the techno-revolution is upon us, making possible amazing things that soon will be routine. Some of us will rise up and embrace the changes—while others will fall backward—trying to hold on to what they've always known in order to avoid overwhelm.

Whether we will take the risks, embrace the changes, and enjoy the sweet rewards is a decision every one of us will make. But to "stay the same" is *not to stay the same.*

It's a fact that life will pass you by if you don't flow with it. As someone told me once, it doesn't matter if we're on the right track. If we're not moving fast enough the train will run us over.

Conditioning is what keeps us stuck.

Why does 95% of our population in these United States die broke—right *here* in the world's richest country? How is that *possible*? Our conditioning tells us, "If I get an education and a good job, I'll be okay."

Not so. Update your file. That era's gone. I heard a few days ago that most employees will change careers—not jobs, *careers*—seven times during their lifetime. And the ranks of the *self*-employed are growing astronomically as the downsizing continues in corporate America. So, the way I see it, in this fast paced and changing world, you're on your own. A corporation won't adopt you. And if you think they have, you might want to think again.

There's one thing you can count on, though. There's something you'll be every single day for the rest of your life, regardless of what else you are. You'll be a consumer.

Whether or not that income stream you're creating is one you'll choose to share in is a personal decision. Some will. Some won't.

But it's a choice that will have major consequences.

The difference between those who do, and those who don't, will not be an external one. It doesn't matter if you're young or old, educated or uneducated, short or tall, rich or poor, sick or well. This business model doesn't exclude anyone.

The only one who can exclude you—is yourself.

I almost did that. I thought I was too busy. I thought a single parent couldn't do it. I thought the odds of my success were less because I was a woman. I didn't think the people that I knew would understand it—and I was absolutely certain that I could not explain it to them.

But one thing saved me. I listened to someone else's story. I met some people who were willing to share what they'd experienced. Some of them had started out with less than I had—but they'd made it work, and they were tasting the rewards of freedom. Some of them were still shy. Some of them were really funny. I listened to them tell their stories sort of like a kid listens to a fairy tale. Just hoping it was true, and wondering if—maybe—I could do it too.

Here's what I found out. If we want to rise past our conditioning, we're going to need some serious help. We aren't going to make it on our own. Our conditioning will pull us down if we don't have another something to hang on to.

The parents I worked with as a social worker did great when I was helping them. The class was opening up new possibilities—giving them more options, new ways of thinking and behaving that would make them happier. As long as that input was feeding them, their lives got better.

But when the class was over, that was it. There were no monthly seminars or training sessions to strengthen their awareness and resolve. There were no teams to build their self-esteem, no one to call on when they were feeling weak and those old worn out programs were returning. There wasn't any System to support them. So most of them— just didn't make it.

So what's the difference between those who make it—and those who don't? It's a mental difference. It's what you do inside your head...the thoughts you listen to.

The great news is regardless of your background or your circumstances you don't have to be a slave to your conditioning. You can have the life you want. You can be free. You can be rich. You can be happier than you have ever dreamed you could be.

I know because I've done it. Okay, well, I wouldn't say I'm rich yet. I mean, some of the people I have worked with in this business make six figures every single *month*—which isn't something I've accomplished yet. It's still in the future for me. But that's what's amazing. It's in the future for me. And that makes the future something very different from what it used to be.

It's in your mind. Every bit of it. The past. The future. What you've thought is what has made your life the way it is today. What you do now is up to you. Either your conditioning will make your future like your past—or you will take advantage of a system that's designed to help you rise above it and create the life you want.

Some will. Some won't. But I definitely wouldn't call it a so-what. Because what hangs on it—is everything.

Chapter Five

Are You Your Own
Best Customer?

(or are you embezzling from yourself?)

**Unreturned loyalty is not
loyalty, but foolishness.**

Five

It's crazy, isn't it? All these years we've been so loyal to this store or that, this brand or that brand. Think of all the money you've been spending. Maybe you're a new consumer, just now taking on your own life as a responsible adult. Or maybe you've been doing it for years. Here's the bottom line: *How much profit do you think those brick and mortar stores are going to share with you?*

How's it gone so far? What checks have they sent you? Ever got one from Sam Walton? Haven't you been loyal to his stores for years? How about those places at the mall you frequent? No profit sharing checks from them so far? Hmm. Could it be your loyalty is just a one way street?

Without a doubt.

Most of us shop here and there and everywhere, scattering our financial favors hither and yon. We have our favorite stores, of course. They get a few more of our pennies than the others do. We make their sales and clip their coupons. We take them our money and take home our goodies. And that's where it stops.

Maybe your children want to go to college. How about checking with your favorite stores to see if they'll contribute to their college fund? Give it a shot. Why not? Haven't you supported them for all these years? Oh, you don't think it works that way? You're right. It doesn't.

So, let's say you start your own Internet business so you can extract some profit for yourself. Excellent idea. Intelligent shoppers catch the drift once you explain it to them, and they join you. Pretty soon you've got a group of proactive consumers who have a new view of their future. They know that what's ahead is going to be a whole lot better than what's behind them. And they're excited. So are you.

You set up your Home Advisor online so you can see exactly how to redirect your spending and how much money you'll save in the process (not to mention the convenience!) Everybody on your team is setting up theirs as well. Every family has their own individual needs, so they get what they want. But everything counts.

What a great way to create income—shopping from yourself!!

But one day it happens. You're walking through the mall (just getting your exercise, of course) when you see it. Something you've been thinking of ordering is right there—and OMG, it's on sale. Your conditioning suddenly kicks in and hijacks your brain. You feel compelled to march into that store and take advantage of that sale!

Believe me, I understand. I did it too—until one day it dawned on me that by taking advantage of that sale I was actually stealing from myself, and not just myself—but from my whole team! Every time I bought something through my own business, I wasn't the only one who got credit for it. We're a team. And it's what we're all creating together that makes the difference. I'm not out there by myself anymore.

That's a discipline of thought—and habit—that takes some time to master. But the faster you can do it, the better off you are. Why? Because you are the leader in your business whether you're aware of it, or not. And whatever you do, the others tend to duplicate.

"Monkey see—monkey do!" Remember how we shouted that at each other back when we were kids? I guess we're all still children in some ways, copying each other and vehemently denying that we are. But hey—we are! That's how conditioning works. But if we *recondition* ourselves to master our buying habits and put our money where it can create a future for us, we will have one that's remarkable.

If not, we'll have the future pretty much everybody else out there is going to wind up with. I think it will be a lot like the one we've had already.

So, who wants a change?

Say, "*Aye!*"

Chapter Six

The Feminine Mystique and Profit

*How is it female dollars are
so powerful? Because there
are so many of them*

Six

Who spends the most money in America? Statistically, the female population wins that ribbon. (Why do I feel all the guys groaning in ratification of that fact?) Hey, think of this: If it weren't for us girls, most of you guys would probably be satisfied living in a shack by a river with a gun and a dog! It's our female influence that elevates your lot in life!)

Okay, and your workload too. What can I say? But we've been taking more than our fair share of that these days. Not just at home—but in the office too. Lots of families have two incomes only because both spouses slug it out all day in their various work places. And when you finally get back home, how much energy do you have left to share with the kids and with each other?

Not so much. I remember those days. Except I didn't have a spouse to help me out. One income. Two kids. And there are lots of single parents who have it tougher than I did. In fact, I read not too long ago that single female parents represent the new poverty segment in our country. What a dubious distinction.

Anyway, I think there's something vital we need to understand about women and money. Facts are that we control most of the cash flow out there. Men buy a *few* things more than we do—like electronic gadgets, for example. (Now I feel the women groaning.) But women are the ones, primarily, that buy the household stuff—things the family uses up that you have to buy again next month. It's those everyday consumables that made Wal-Mart the largest retail store alive—over 100 billion every year! And *women* are the ones controlling all that cash.

I had a meeting with a businessman sometime ago. I explained to him what we were doing. He got it.

He talked to several other businessmen immediately. Before long there were almost 20 of them, buzzing like a hive of bees, excited about their new joint venture. Only one problem. They didn't tell their wives. Or if they did, it didn't quite go over with a bang.

I'll give you a hint. Wives tend to resist husbands they believe are bringing home another thing to add to their already too multi-tasked lives. Or sometimes they assume their husbands are just going through a "phase." And they plan to stay as far from it as possible until it runs its course.

Whatever the case was, their wives were not enrolled in the idea. So guess what loyal customers these guys developed? Zip. Without the women on board, nothing happened. A great car may look gorgeous sitting in the driveway—but face it, without gasoline, that baby is a statue. It's going nowhere.

It's like that with this too. Consumer Power is a great looking concept, but it won't go anywhere without the gas. It wouldn't matter if a thousand people thought it was a great idea—if they kept on funneling all their money through the other system, there'd be no profit stream to draw from.

And since it is a fact that women control most of that type buying, it's crucial that we take the time to win their loyalty. Women, like the rest of human kind, are creatures of habit. Conditioning tells us what to do and when. Unless somebody goes to the trouble of showing us how much power we have, and what can actually be done with it, we're not interested in changing our buying habits.

If we don't understand what's happening here, we won't support it.

But if we do—hey, if we really do—*look out!* I mean it. Once a woman really gets the picture, that's when she gets dangerous. Because a woman hates (and I mean *hates*) hanging her heart out a limb of hopes and dreams her husband gives her when he tells her he is going to do this—only to have those hopes come crashing down around her.

Here's some advice: Don't promise your woman great things and then hit the armchair every night sipping your Diet Coke in front of the TV. I mean it. You'll have one witchy woman on your hands. If you want her to be your #1 best customer, *you'd* better be your #1 best UFO. Make something happen. Share the information. Build the group. I'm giving you fair warning. Don't say I didn't tell you.

The feminine mystique is worth over a billion dollars. (Ask the Walton family.)

And all we have to do is let our women in on what is possible if they are willing to shift paradigms. But then—once they understand it, you better follow through. If it doesn't take off like a rocket, that won't matter. What will impress her is a true commitment. Women like commitment. And they like results. Isn't it amazing how those two always seem to show up hand in hand?

If you're a woman who is single, like myself, take *these* words to heart: **You can do it**. It's great to have a man to help you. But if you don't, there's still your coaching team to count on. And you'll create your own team too, and that will open up a whole new world for you.

I have friends around the world. I really do. Lonely—I *never* am. Life is wonderful. And to think it all began because I finally decided I might be better off learning to buy from my own business—and sharing that option. Man, oh man! Was I right, or what!

So here's my bugle call: *Female consumer power—unite!*

The future belongs to us!

Chapter Seven

A Diversity of Dreams

*What if the most valuable thing
you own is something you have
not yet given birth to?*

Seven

Not everybody wants the same thing. But we all want something. Somewhere in the heart of every human being is a powerful stream of energy. We call it *desire.* A proverb in the Bible says, "Hope delayed makes the heart sick; but *desire,* when it comes, is a tree of life."

When you're really going after something you want, you feel *alive.* Whether you're an athlete going for the gold or a lover courting your mate, it's the energy of *wanting* that drives us forward, gives us hope. Human beings at their best are always chasing a dream.

So what's your dream? Can you remember? We've all had one. Some of us have buried ours and tried to forget it. Some of us have trivialized it and told ourselves we didn't want it anyway. Some of us have tried to live it, but we've had to pare it down to fit our resources. But no matter what you've done with it, your dream is still alive.

How do I know? Because you're reading this right now. I think you know this isn't a generic message. It's very personal. It's a confidential message to you from your dream.

"I'm still alive...what will you do with me?"

That's a serious question. Because if you abort your dream, you may just be aborting your whole mission—the reason that you're here. What are you here for, anyway? Surely not just to drive to work a million times, and keep the oil changed, and pay the light bill when it's due. Surely it's more than that. What is it?

I believe your purpose and your dream grow from the same stem. And if you sever one, you will destroy the other. So it's not a casual question.

"But what if all I want is just to get the debts paid off, and buy a car that works, and get a home with a backyard so the kids can have somewhere to play? Is that a dream?" Sure. It's like a tender shoot coming out of the ground. You're looking at the part that you can see. But underneath, where you can't see it, there's a root. Just dig a little deeper and you'll find it.

Think about it. Why do you want to get those debts paid off? What's that about? Could it be about having integrity? Self respect? Could it be about being responsible and financially independent? And why do you want a better car—and house with a back yard? What's at the root of that? Look and see. Security. Safety. A desire to create a nurturing environment so you can raise a happy family with lots of great memories?

Exactly.

So it's not really *about* stuff, now is it? I finally figured that out. Even the stuff you want isn't about the stuff itself. It's part of a picture you're trying to create; an experience you're looking for. It's a symbol of a feeling you want to have about yourself—and about your world.

That's important to understand. It's not selfish to want "stuff" as long you understand what it really is. It's a tool, an instrument. Its true value is in the purpose that lies behind it. That's the real issue. What do you want it *for*?

A friend of mine was told to get a dream to get her motivated. She taped pictures of expensive cars and gorgeous houses on her refrigerator door, and tried to want them. But somehow she couldn't get a fire going. Nothing sparked. So she found some other pictures; motor homes, log cabins—those were better. But nothing quite took hold.

Then one day she suddenly remembered what she had told me years before when I'd asked her casually what she'd do if she should win the lottery. She'd described a ranch she'd like to build, a haven for abused or neglected children and unwanted animals. She described it in detail. "Kids and animals nurture each other", she told me. They can heal each others' hurts. She'd name the ranch "Catherine's Haven," in honor of her mother.

As she unearthed that dream only a week or two ago, the tears welled up. Now she understood.

Catherine's Haven was her dream. Not cars or houses, not even motorhomes—"although the motorhomes do have to go somewhere on the list," she told me with a grin. "But kids and animals—they stir my heart. Catherine's Haven isn't supposed to be a passing fantasy. It's my dream. But I can't build it without money.

And that's going to take a lot more than my job can ever give me."

Suddenly she knew *exactly* why she had to do this business. She'd found her dream again, and proved yet one more time that "desire, when it comes, is a tree of life."

So whatever your dream may be, it's worth uncovering. Get it down off that back shelf you put it on. Unwrap it. Brush off the dust of disappointment and frustration; all those discouragements that have kept it covered up inside you. You see, your dream isn't just your dream. Your dream is who you are.

It *is* you. So what you're worth is what it's worth. How much is that?

Chapter Eight

The Three Levels of Energy

Up and down and all around...
Is that all there is to life?

Eight

Okay, what if it's true that everybody has a dream? Let's say you decide to dust it off and get excited about chasing it? Who's to say that motivation's going to last? I mean, which of us hasn't made some big decision to quit smoking, or lose weight, or get in shape, or read more books—only to wander off the path, not to return for months?

That's what gets discouraging. It causes us to doubt ourselves. It makes us wonder, even when we do see a possibility, whether we can trust ourselves to follow through on it. In fact, a lot of us are pretty sure we won't. We've fallen off the motivational wagon too many times before. We have a track record of interrupted attempts at lots of things. So why should we try again and add another disappointment to the list?

Too honest for you? Maybe it's time we went ahead and got that honest on the front end—rather than covering up our eyes with good intentions and blindly falling into all the same ditches we've been in before. What do you think?

I know I've ridden that motivational roller coaster too many times. Up and down.

Up and down. Two steps forward, three steps back. It can be a rat race all its own. So how do you get off the rollercoaster and keep the ball rolling in the right direction till you get the result you're looking for?

Good question. Not many people ever ask it. You're already in the upper regions of successful thinkers just probing into that dilemma. Most folks get discouraged and settle in at mediocrity. Their conditioning keeps them from going very far outside the lines—or if they wander temporarily, it keeps them coming back where they "belong."

What I've found out is that there are three levels of energy that drive people. And what their life becomes is actually determined by the one they choose. If you can determine what level of energy you're living at right now, you can look and see where you want to go from there, or if you're happy staying where you are.

The lowest level of energy is Maintenance. That's the every day energy level where you find most folks. They go to work, do their job, eat lunch, go back to work, go home, do the dinner and the kid thing, go to church, watch TV, pick up the cleaning, fix the car, pay the bills—you know the routine. Just keeping things steady. Status quo. Every now and then they do something special just to spice things up. Maybe a movie or a night out. A church retreat. A ski trip in the mountains for a day or two. Something to look forward to.

If you graph the energy at this lower level, it's a circle. Home to work. Work to home. Round and round, with a few blips here and there so it won't be too boring. It doesn't take a lot of spark to keep it going. It runs on inertia. What's in motion tends to stay in motion and conditioning keeps you in the lines. You're part of the tribe. You're normal.

The second level of energy is Motivation. You have a goal. You want to accomplish something. While the first level of energy is about maintaining, this level is about improving things. That's when you decide you'll get in shape, drop some weight, feel good again. So you join a fitness club. You're revved. You work out. You're sore. It hurts. You go again. Maybe you even keep it up awhile. A week, two weeks. But something interrupts. Your mother comes to visit. The work load doubles at the office. There is a crisis at home. You catch a cold. Whatever it is, you interrupt your motion toward your goal... and somehow, guess what? You never reinstate it.

That's the rollercoaster. Up and down. If you graph this level of energy, that's exactly what it looks like. Up and down. Like the stock market. Highs and lows. Maybe that's why 95% of all investors never get ahead financially. They don't stay the course. They ride the roller coaster for awhile, and finally get off. When you get off, you lose.

The third level of energy is Inspiration. Whereas the first two levels of energy revolve around *you*, it's not true here. Maintenance and motivation are about getting something for yourself. Maintenance is about your survival and comfort. Motivation is about improvement and personal goals. But Inspiration is another *kind* of energy. It's about giving, not getting. It's about making a difference. It's not really about comfort or improvement for yourself—although they often show up too, more as a byproduct than a focus.

If you draw a graph of Inspirational energy it looks like the growth curve of a successful business. It begins slowly, gradually—then gains momentum till it goes straight up. If you've ever seen a launch of the space shuttle you've seen exactly how it works.

Ninety percent of the fuel is spent in the first few seconds—and gets the shuttle only about twelve feet off the ground. It takes the rest of the fuel to get it on out through the atmosphere. But after that, its own momentum carries it around the earth as many times as we desire—with no fuel at all.

That's how it works. It won't take any extra energy for you to keep that space shuttle you call your life safely on the ground. That's level one. And most people live there. Only a minority take their lives to level two. If they do, it will take most of their energy just getting twelve feet off the ground. That's Motivation, level two. And most of them will fall back, over and over. Some will quit trying, and decide it isn't worth it.

But there is another level of Energy in life. And when you decide to go for that one, everything you ever dreamed will be there for you. The biggest dream inside you, the dream of making great things happen for someone *besides* you—that's the dream God gave you. And that's the dream that lives at level three. It's the one that will fulfill your mission. It's the reason you came here. And if you miss it, you will have missed your life.

So how do you go from one, to two, to three? What's the process? It's simple, really.

First, you decide to. No one changes their level of energy without a decision. It won't creep up on you by accident. It will be a conscious, volitional move on your part. You just decide you're not satisfied with where you are; you can be more.

Second, you connect with people who live there already. Obviously, they won't be the majority. But you'll know who they are. One of them probably gave you this book. And if you hang around with us, you'll meet quite a few more. But we are definitely the minority. And that's okay.

Third, you feed yourself at that level of energy. You filter your input. Turn off the radio and plug in an audio that teaches you something. Turn off the television and play a video that makes you think, or fills you with hope. Turn off the music that doesn't lift you up and put on some that does. Get rid of the toxins in your mind. The negative self talk, the "I can't do it's."

Replace that with positive. Listen constantly to the ones who have achieved what you are shooting for. They did it. So can you. The space shuttle really does fly. But first you have to get it through the atmosphere.

Fourth, you give it away. The twelfth step of Alcoholics Anonymous is one of the most crucial steps in keeping recovering alcoholics sober. It's the "giving away" step. Helping others who want their sobriety to find the path. No one stays at level two or level three without sharing it. *You will stay at the level of energy you give away.* It can't be otherwise.

That's it.

Take this to heart, and it will change your life. I guarantee it. Jesus said once, "Take My yoke upon you, and learn from Me, for My yoke is easy and My burden is light." I always wondered what he meant by that. Now I know. He lived at Level Three. His space shuttle was way on out there. And that's where we can be too—if we will make the trip.

It's the life we were born to live. Whether we live it or not—is up to us.

Chapter Nine

A Global Family

*An idea that starts at the top and goes down
is authority driven—coercing many,
and benefiting a few.
An idea that starts at the bottom
and goes up is the child of free men—
and a blessing to all.*

Nine

Okay, maybe it's naive, but I believe the world can work. I really do. I believe if something works for some of us, it can work for many. And if it works for many, it can work for lots. And if it works for lots—it can work for everybody. Is that too simple?

I read in an important Book once that "a little child shall lead them." Maybe you've read that too. I think sometimes we over-complicate things. We assume everybody has to think like we do for the world to work. Well, that may be a long time, given that we have a few million cultures and religions and personal histories to deal with. So if everybody has to think alike before the world can work, we're up a creek.

But what if that's not it? Maybe what has to happen is for each of us to find our dream—the one God gave us—and decide to go for it. What if we all have a piece of the world's puzzle buried in our hearts—and until we un-bury it, our piece will be missing?

My job's not to ask what my neighbors are doing with their dream. It's not to ask what someone on the other side of the world is doing. My job is to ask what I am doing with mine. Once I become committed to my own, then I can turn around and help you with yours. And *that's* how the world can work.

It's not complicated. It never was.

I remember coming to one of my first major events after I got started in this business. People were lining up for blocks. I couldn't believe it. When I finally got inside the auditorium, music was playing. Everyone was celebrating. Some folks were dancing in the aisles, just having fun. People were high-fiving each other and everybody was excited. The energy flowing in that room was just short of electric. I couldn't have described it then, but it was definitely not a Level one!

I couldn't even get onto the bottom floor. It was too full. By the time I got there we were going to the balcony. I remember standing at the railing watching everybody dancing down below. "This isn't like a business meeting," I thought to myself. "It's more like something else...what is it?" I was flashing back to my sociology class in college. Our professor talked about the power of grass roots movements—changes in society that came not from authorities or governments. Changes that start out at the bottom and grow from there. A grass roots movement starts with every day people who get a vision and move *out* of Level one.

That's what I felt there in that place. Suddenly I understood what I was viewing. "But where's it going?" I thought. "What's it about?" I knew that every grass roots movement in history had accomplished something. They addressed major issues and brought about a change in society, starting at the bottom and going to the top. "So what was this one all about?" I wondered. And as I stood there thinking, I already knew.

It's about the redistribution of wealth in the whole world.

I got light headed thinking about it. Every war ever fought was ultimately about that. I remembered that from history. From WWII to the storming of the Bastille in France to the Russian revolution. It was always the same story. The distribution of wealth inequitably has been the catalyst for violence for centuries.

But here was a grass roots movement that had the possibility of reversing that.

Profitable communities, recycling the wealth of their own buying power among themselves. It was, indeed, a revolutionary concept with the power to change the world.

So who would wind up with the wealth in this new paradigm? As I stood looking down there from the balcony, I knew that too. It would be the ones who dared to keep believing in the dream, to step out and risk sharing it with others and giving them hope. The ones who wouldn't give up when the going got rough. The ones who stayed the course, through all the ups and downs of the roller coaster. The ones who kept themselves motivated and inspired.

This wealth would be distributed fairly. Not based on violence or power. It would go to those whose characters were forged in the fire of tenacity and vision, true compassion, and unyielding faith. At last the ones who deserve the wealth—would be the ones who had it.

I remember feeling moved as I heard the music blare and watched the people dance. There was much more here than met the eye. I could feel the heartbeat of a whole new world of possibility: A world that worked.

Since then, I've only grown more sure of it each day. The men and women who began this vision decades ago have passed it on to us. It has changed in form over the years. But like a child, growing from infancy through adolescence, to maturity—every stage has been important.

Where will it go from here? I have no crystal ball. All I have is what you have— my heart, my hopes, my vision, and my faith. But I've decided that it's right. I've decided that it's possible. I've decided that my dream is part of the puzzle that will make the world a better place. And I've decided to go for it.

How hard is it to buy things through my own business? Not hard.

How hard is it to share that possibility with someone else? A little harder. After all, they might not get it.

How hard is it to find my dream? Harder. But if I want to find it, God will help me. He's the one that gave it to me in the first place.

How hard is it to motivate myself? Harder still. Sometimes it requires 90% of my emotional energy to get myself twelve feet off the ground.

How hard is it to get inspired? Hardest of all. You have to penetrate the atmosphere of doubt to make it to that level.

After that—it's easy.

Think about it. The *process* of the business isn't the hard part. It just makes sense. After all, why should you keep on putting all your money through an antiquated distribution system and lose out on the chance to live your dream? (*That's* what would *not* make sense.)

What's hard is the internal journey. (You knew that, didn't you?)

It's not easy to break through your conditioning, and venture out into the never-never land of hopes and dreams until you find the one you're here for. But I can tell you this: It's an adventure much more exciting than Lewis and Clark could have imagined.

And even if it's hard, it's worth it.

Let me tell you something that was harder.

What was harder was living a life of quiet desperation with nothing to hope for. What was hard was going to bed at night not knowing what today was all about.

What was hard was telling my children I couldn't be with them—and not knowing when it would be different.

What was hard was living a life of limitation, debt, and endless obligation without dignity or peace.

So do I think *this* path is hard? I have to chuckle. Not really. At least there's a trail to follow. You won't be blazing it yourself. And there'll be lots of us beside you. You won't be alone. And even if we're still a vast minority—a million of us in a world that's several billion strong—we're at the root of a new movement. One that has an honest chance to change the world.

And what could be more fun than that?

ACKNOWLEDGEMENTS
No one makes a journey alone.

My deepest thanks goes to all those who have mentored me in this great industry. To Dr. David and Melissa Hullender, who introduced me to the paradigm that opened my eyes and changed my life. To Mike Jakubik and Gerry Betterman who made the original printing of this book possible. And to my newest partners, Carol Parker and Kathy Gaughan, whose visionary enthusiasm launched a reprint—because they believe it's time.

Special thanks also to those who have been friends along the way—too many to name—and especially to my closest friend and assistant, Angela Ferrell, without whose support and encouragement I would not have dared to do many of the things I now attempt.

And of course, to God—who gives us all a dream to light the way.

About the Author

Susan Frederick is a single parent who has fought the battle for financial freedom in what has become a two-income family world. Having owned her own small advertising agency, she eventually became a business broker. Evaluating businesses and assisting their transfer to new owners gave her an insider's look at the world of traditional business. It was with this background and perspective that she reviewed a developing business model—a phenomenon referred to as "partnering."

With that business model as her financial lever, within two years she was able to retire from business brokerage and return home to raise her two children and enjoy her life. "The secret to financial freedom is residual income," she explains. "The problem is that most of us don't really have a grip on what that is—and we certainly don't know how to create it."

Using the partnering approach, she asserts, is the way anyone can create a passive income without the time and capital demands that are required for traditional businesses. The only qualification necessary is consumer status—a qualification every monetarily functional adult has already achieved. "It is the re-routing of existing cashflow and the reorganization of profits to include consumers that creates this kind of income," she explains. "All you really have to do is be smart enough to understand it—and willing to reposition yourself as part of the profit loop."

"I wasn't looking to get rich," she says. "I was looking to get free. People get financially free when they can pay their bills without having to go to work anymore. That's all I wanted. And that's what I got. Everything else is gravy."

Susan makes her home in Grapevine, Texas. She is a freelance writer and has spoken at conferences around the world as an advocate and teacher of the partnering concept.

Facebook Page:
www.facebook.com/susan.j.frederick

Made in the USA
Lexington, KY
17 August 2018